SOFTWARE
CONST
BRICK

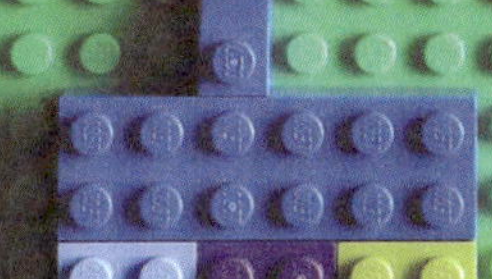

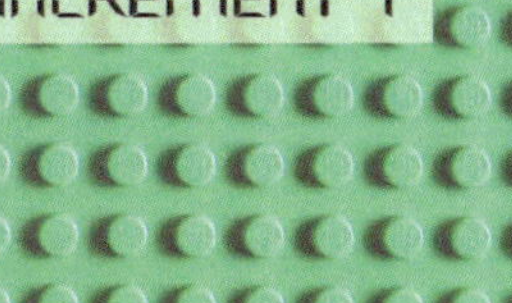

INCREMENT 1

DMITRY VOSTOKOV

Software Construction Brick by Brick, Increment 1: Using LEGO® to Teach Software Architecture, Design, Implementation, Internals, Diagnostics, Debugging, Testing, Integration, and Security

Published by OpenTask, Republic of Ireland

OpenTask books and magazines are available through booksellers and distributors worldwide. For further information or comments, send requests to press@opentask.com.

A CIP catalog record for this book is available from the British Library.

ISBN-13: 978-1912636709 (Paperback)

Revision 1.01 (May 2020)

Preface

My interest in using LEGO® for teaching software internals goes back to Memory Dump Analysis Anthology[1], Volume 9b,[2] where I explained heap corruption, and illustrated linked lists, stacks, packed and unpacked structures. Later I applied the same technique for depicting trace and log analysis patterns[3]. My LEGO® modeling skills got a boost when I invented a baseplate representation of chemical structures[4]. Then I got an idea to represent machine learning topics using bricks[5], and even abstract mathematics such as graphs and category theory[6]. After that, I recalled my usage of colored block diagrams to illustrate pointers[7], Unified Modeling Language to represent Windows operating system internals such as drivers and their interaction[8] and colored UML diagrams for debugging and diagnostic software construction patterns[9]. So all that fused into these series of short books (increments) you are reading now.

The first increment covers memory, memory addresses, pointers, program loading, kernel and user spaces, virtual process space, memory isolation, virtual and physical memory, memory paging, memory dump types.

---

1 https://www.dumpanalysis.org/advanced-software-debugging-reference

2 https://www.dumpanalysis.org/Memory+Dump+Analysis+Anthology+Volume+9b

3 https://www.dumpanalysis.org/lego-log-analysis

4 https://www.opentask.com/lego-baseplate-representation-of-chemical-structure

5 https://www.dumpanalysis.org/machine-learning-brick-by-brick-series

6 https://www.dumpanalysis.org/visual-category-theory

7 https://www.dumpanalysis.org/SoftwareConstruction/PointerInternalsDraft2015.pdf

8 https://www.dumpanalysis.org/advanced-windows-memory-dump-analysis-book

9 https://www.dumpanalysis.org/blog/index.php/debugware-patterns/

We represent computer memory as a linear sequence of memory cells.

Every cell contains some value. Empty cells contain 0 value. But in our representation, white cells may also contain unspecified values.

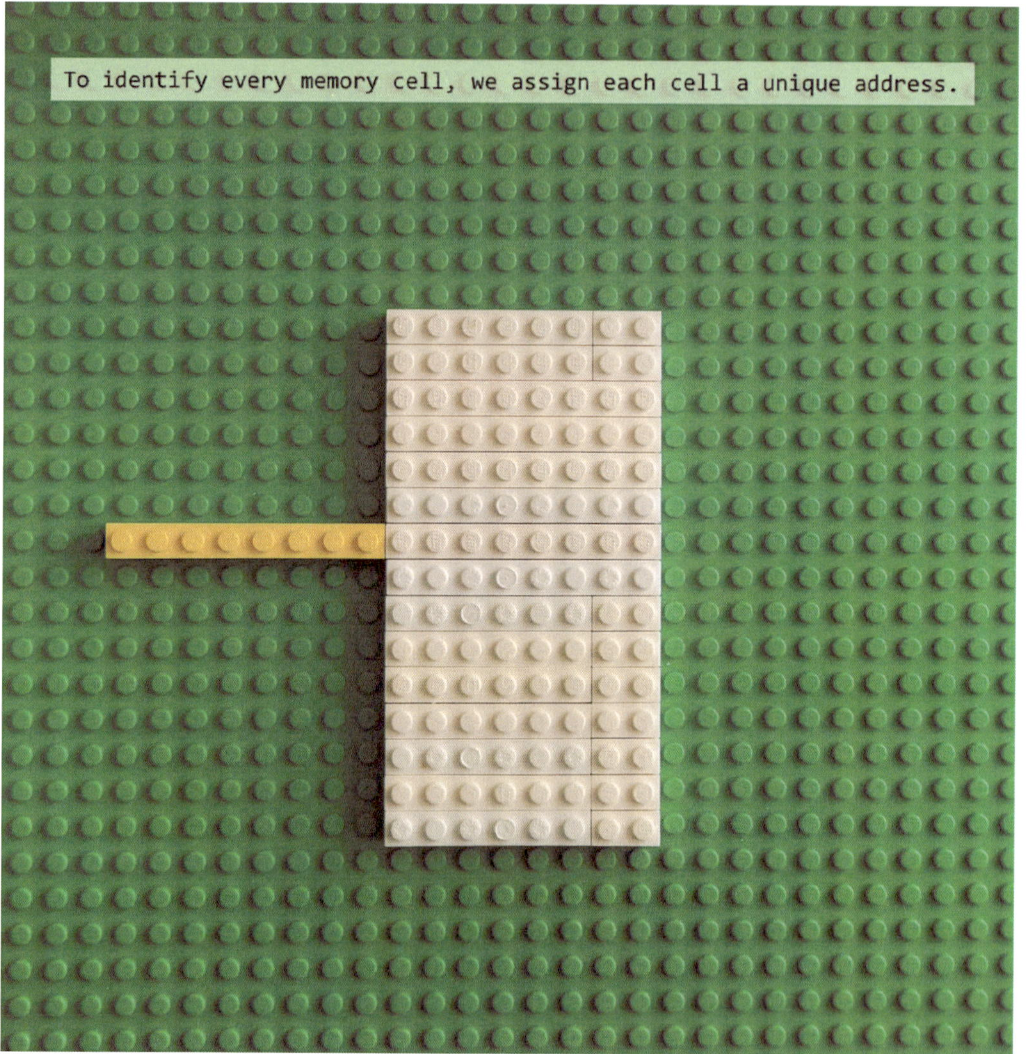
To identify every memory cell, we assign each cell a unique address.

Usually, addresses have increasing values highlighting the linear nature of memory.

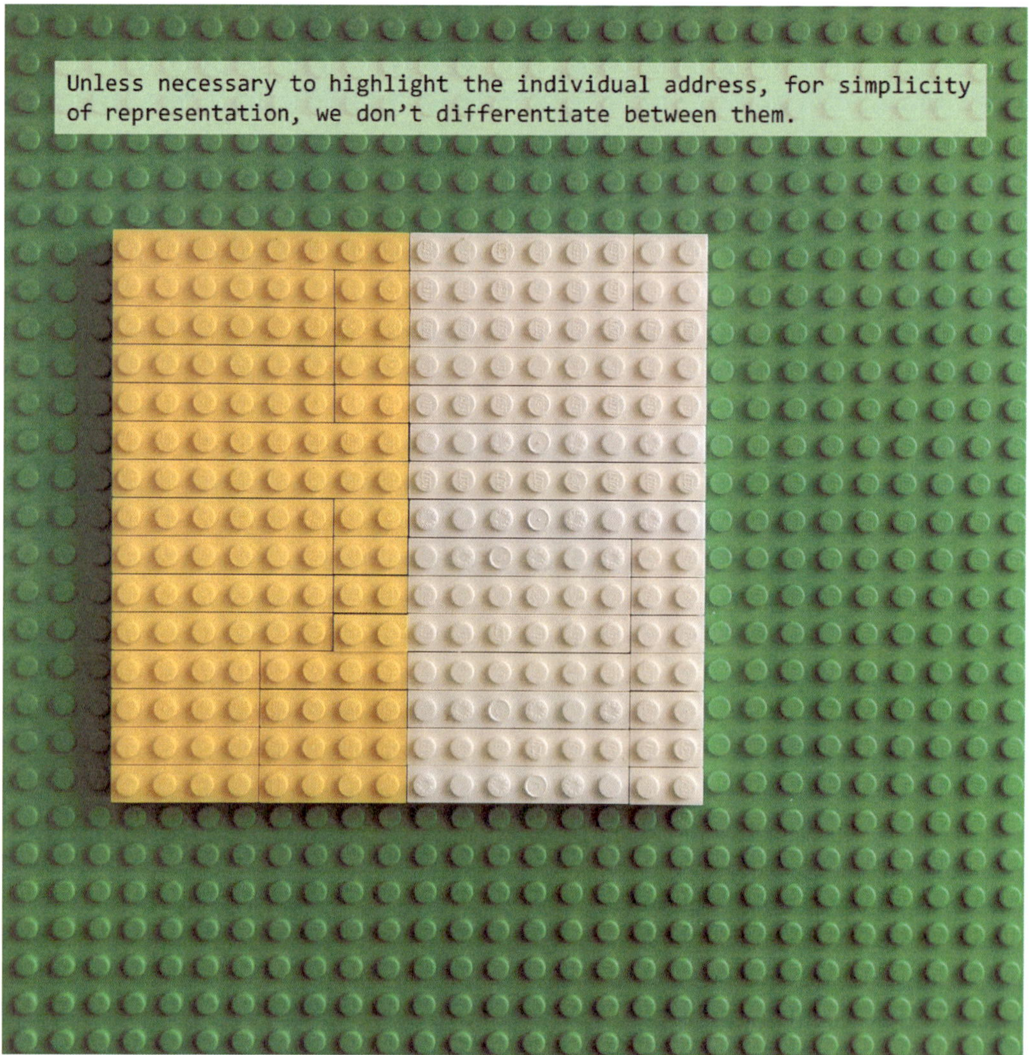
Unless necessary to highlight the individual address, for simplicity of representation, we don’t differentiate between them.

Programs from secondary storage like disks are loaded into memory where there may be gaps between individual program sections or modules. Some sections may also expand in memory.

A memory address may be stored in a memory cell.

The address of that cell is called a pointer.

The value of a pointer is the address of a memory cell it points to.

Some pointers may point to itself.

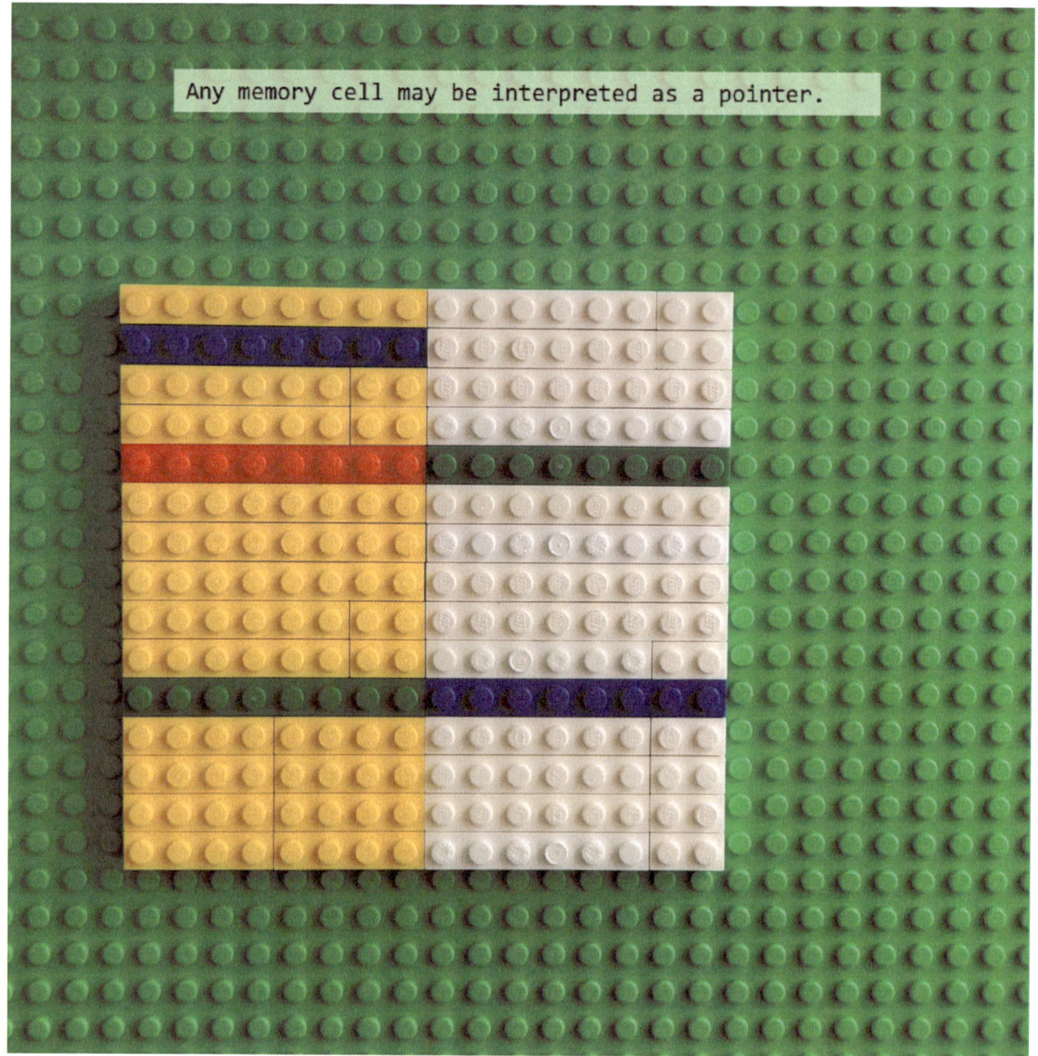
Any memory cell may be interpreted as a pointer.

And, pointers may be linked pointing to random memory locations.

Usually, memory is divided into two distinct classes: kernel memory (red addresses) and user (program) memory (blue addresses).
Both are well isolated.
kernel space
user space

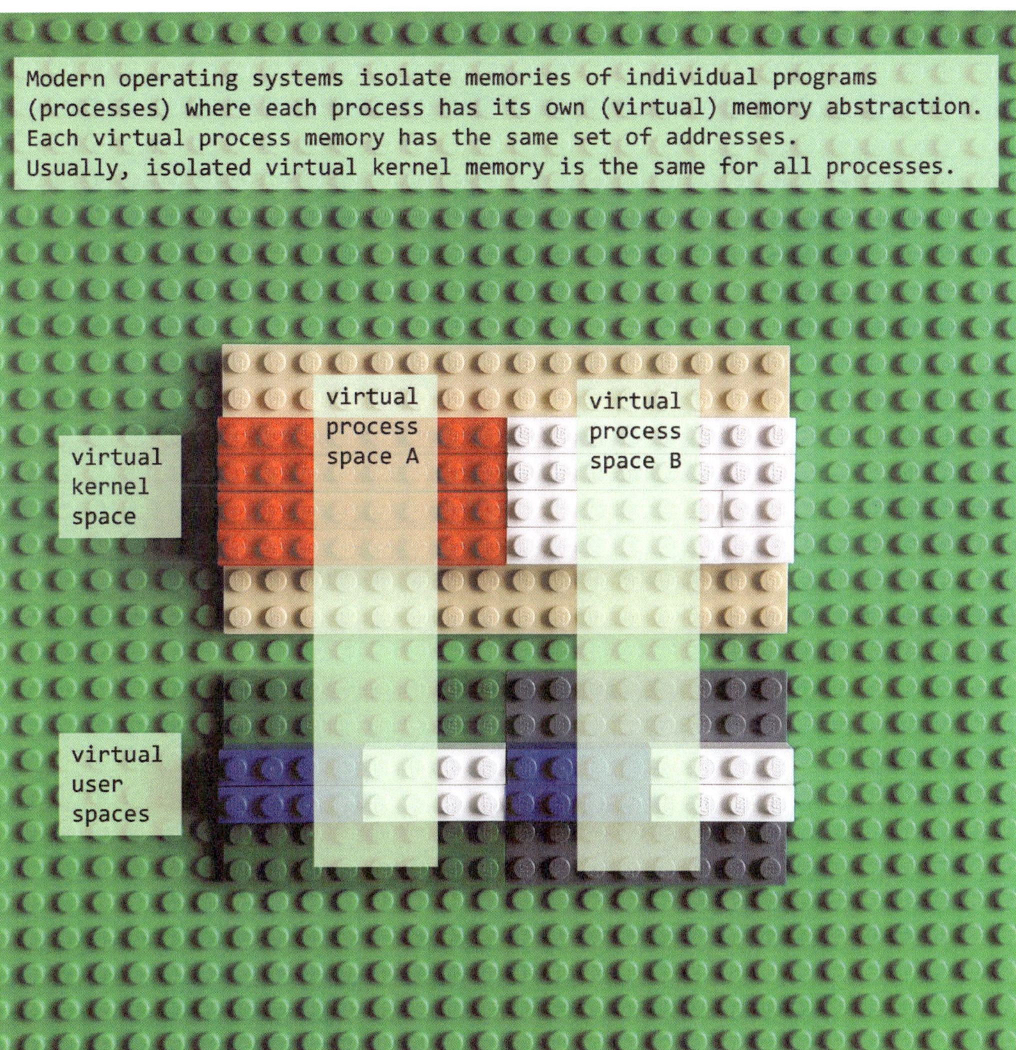
Modern operating systems isolate memories of individual programs
(processes) where each process has its own (virtual) memory abstraction.
Each virtual process memory has the same set of addresses.
Usually, isolated virtual kernel memory is the same for all processes.
virtual
process
space A
virtual
process
space B
virtual
kernel
space
virtual
user
spaces

The values from virtual memory abstraction of all processes need to be stored in the physical memory of a computer for execution.

But not all virtual memory cells fit in physical memory.

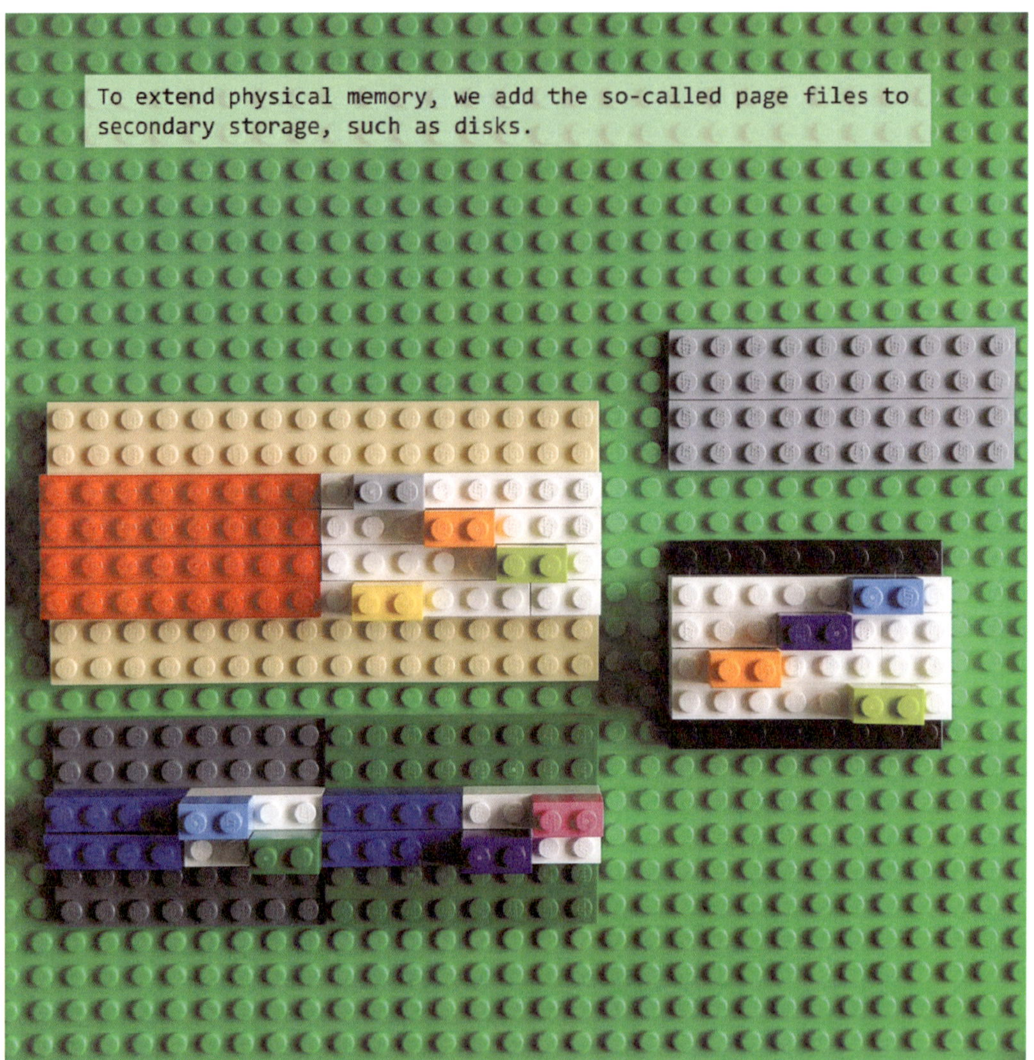
To extend physical memory, we add the so-called page files to secondary storage, such as disks.

To make room for new virtual cells in physical memory, we temporarily save the values of some cells in a page file (memory paging).

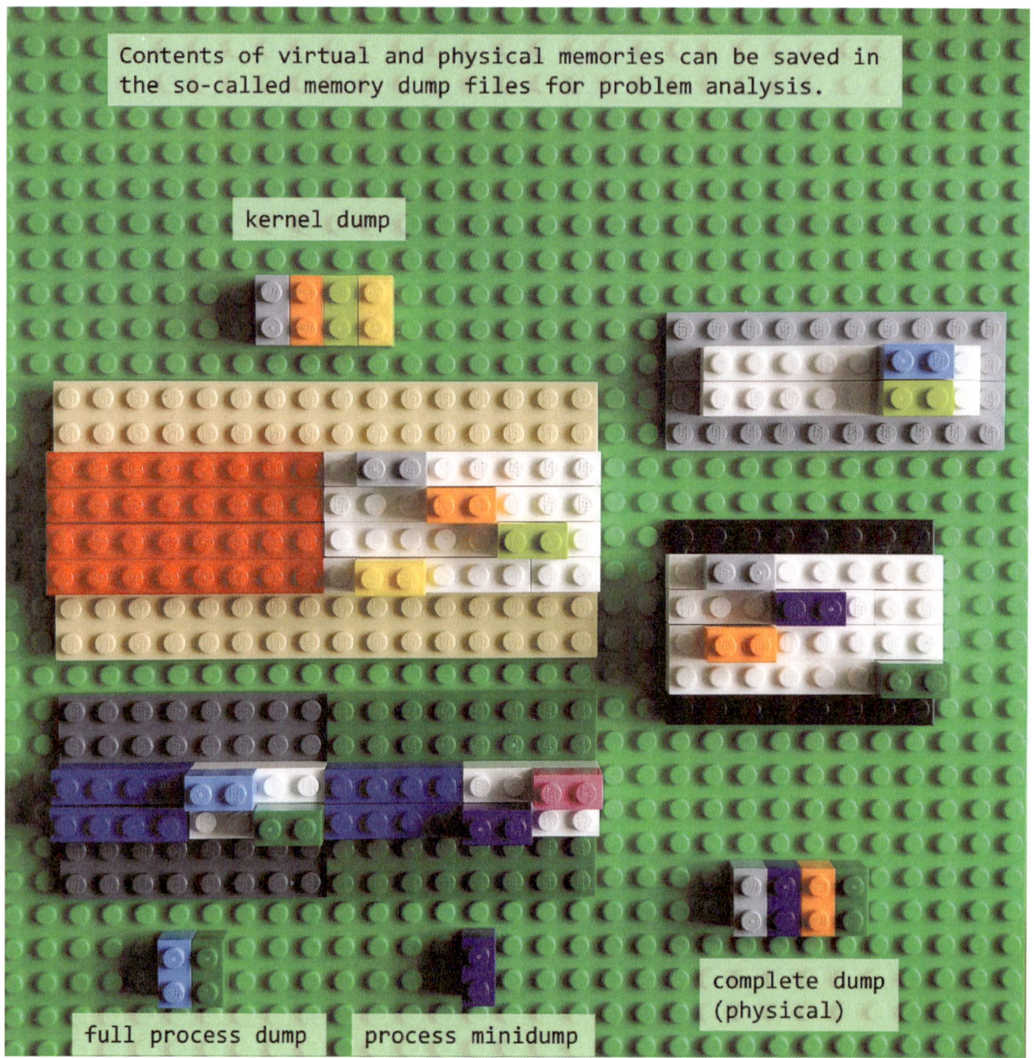
Contents of virtual and physical memories can be saved in the so-called memory dump files for problem analysis.
kernel dump
complete dump (physical)
full process dump
process minidump

www.ingramcontent.com/pod-product-compliance
Ingram Content Group UK Ltd.
Pitfield, Milton Keynes, MK11 3LW, UK
UKRC031356070726
13610UKWH00008BA/12

* 9 7 8 1 9 1 2 6 3 6 7 0 9 *